Aquariums   Sharks
Pet Sharks and Shark Fish Care

The Complete Owners Guide

Keeping freshwater and marine sharks and shark fish in home aquariums.

Shark care, facts, tanks, equipment, where to buy, health, habitat, breeding, food and diseases all covered.

Alex Halton

Published by ROC Publishing 2013

Foreword

Aquascaping is about world building. The process of creating an aquarium and stocking it with fish engages the aquarist in designing a microcosm of the underwater universe.

We can only visit the real version of that world by breathing oxygen from a tank for a few minutes or by staying safely encased in steel, peering out through tiny portals.

Studies have proven that watching fish swimming in a beautifully designed tank can lower blood pressure, reduce stress, and cure insomnia.

There is something hypnotic and other worldly in the fluid scene playing out on the other side of the glass. The effect of watching fish on humans is so powerful that Alzheimer's patients eat more and display fewer aggressive physical behaviors when aquariums are placed in their dining area.

For some aquarium enthusiasts, the ultimate goal is owning a home tank large enough to house some species of shark. These magnificent creatures have been kept in public aquariums since the 1860s, but now it is possible for hobbyists to access the level of equipment necessary to successfully keep sharks as pets.

Make no mistake. Keeping a shark in a home tank requires tremendous attention to detail. In this book, we'll discuss a class of freshwater "shark like" fish that, while not true sharks, display the same overall physical appearance as their larger cousins.

Many of these fish are aggressive and even predatory, eating or harassing smaller fish or being so aggressive with one another that only a single member of the species can be kept at a time.

How Big Is Big?

The largest privately-owned reef tank in North America measures 24' long, 10' high, and 10' feet wide (7.31m x 3m x 3m) and holds 20,000 gallons (75,708.2 liters) of water. The enclosure is so massive that volunteer scuba divers help to clean the interior.

The viewing areas are made of 2.5" (6.35 cm) thick acrylic, giving visitors a means to watch the 100-150 fish that live inside.

Some of those specimens are valued at $500 to $1000 (£324 - £648) each. The man who owns the massive tank, dreams of building a bigger one — maybe 80,000 gallons (302,832.9 liters).

The world's biggest water tank for raising fish is located in Singapore. It contains 12 million gallons (45,424,941.4 liters) of water, and is home to 100,000 animals representing 800 species.

It boasts the largest viewing panel in the world as well, 118 feet wide by 27 feet tall (35.9m x 8.2m). The previous record was held by the Georgia Aquarium in Atlanta at 10 million gallons (37,854,117.8 liters).

The most hotly anticipated event at the Singapore installation is the planned offering of interactions between humans and sharks starting sometime in 2013.

Do you have to go to these lengths to have a shark in your life? No. The species discussed in this book, whether shark-like fish or "true" sharks can live in tanks ranging from 50 gallons to 300 gallons (189.27 to 1135.6 liters). That's a price difference for the fisher keeper of roughly $500 to $2000 (£324 - £1296).

Freshwater tanks are, technically, easier than saltwater. However, all aquariums require an understanding of water chemistry, and a degree of monitoring sufficiently complex to have spawned a new generation of sensors and probes controlled by sophisticated computer programs.

Given the expense of the tank, the required equipment, the needed electricity, and even the fish themselves, failing to maintain a tank of this size would be insane.

In fact, the investment on large home aquariums is so great, in both time and money, that most enthusiasts place riders on their homeowners insurance policies. This is to protect themselves against sudden or catastrophic failure of the glass, damage to the home due to aquarium equipment failure, and even the cost of replacing the contents of the tank in the event of a disaster.

The horror stories on discussion forums when things go wrong make it clear why people are willing to pay the premiums on such policies. For example, a fish enthusiast wrote, "About 5 years ago when I had my last saltwater tank set up I had an equipment failure that resulted in about 35 gallons (132.48 liters) of saltwater damaging my wood floors." Luckily, his insurance covered everything, but to protect himself, the man decided to start keeping a smaller tank.

Other aquarists, however, go in completely the opposite direction and simply add more failsafe measures like overflow boxes and sophisticated monitoring devices. The point is? This is a hobby that easily takes on a life of its own.

It's not that unusual to talk to a fish keeper, standing beside a $5000 tank (£3,241) holding 500 gallons (1,892.7 liters) of water who says something like, "I really don't know what happened. I started small, with a 20 gallon (75.7 liters) tank." And, if he's really honest, he's already thinking about moving up to 600 gallons (2,271.25 liters.)

People who take up this hobby invest time, money, and effort to learn how to do what they're doing and do it well. Is it little wonder they'd find keeping a shark, especially a large one, an appealing challenge?

This book is an effort to answer some basic, practical questions for people contemplating making the next step up in their hobby — or for those who are completely new to keeping fish and want to know what they might be getting into.

There are many subjects here that are treated in an introductory sense, like basic water chemistry or cycling a tank. This is a jumping off place for what can easily become a life-long learning process.

People who have successfully been keeping large tanks for years admit they learn something new every day, which is one of the great appeals of owning a big tank — and keeping a complex fish like a shark — in the first place.

You may not ever be able to make your home in the ocean, but you can, with care and commitment, bring a part of the ocean into your life, and with it, one of the world's most fascinating creatures — the shark.

Acknowledgements

Su…you are my inspiration and my motivation.

****

" The Sea, once it casts its spell, holds one in its net of wonder forever "

Jacques-Yves Cousteau

Contents

Chapter 1 - Introduction to Keeping Aquarium Sharks

Sharks are, for many people, fascinating but feared creatures. Before his death, Peter Benchley, the author of "Jaws" regretted that his novel helped to create the popular perception of sharks as monsters.

"Sharks are much more the victims than the villains," Benchley said in a press conference in 2000, as he appealed to the public to support shark conservation efforts.

Regardless of the positive or negative nature of the perception, however, sharks are compelling — so much so, that many people are attracted to the idea of keeping them in home aquariums. Understanding the roots of that desire and what is involved to make it a reality are the purpose of this book.

The Perception of Sharks in Popular Culture

In 2011, Kevin Zelnio, a writer for DeapSeaNews.com posed a question on Twitter. "In 140 or less why are you (or are you not) fascinated by #sharks."

In the story he subsequently wrote, he quoted people who talked about the grace and beauty of these majestic creatures.

They "look like they own the place" enthused one fan. Another said, "They're ancient, and one of the last things left on earth that puts us lower on the food chain. Gotta respect that."

But the one word that was used over and over again was "awesome!"

Very few of us can afford to host the kind of shark tank that would comfortably house the magnificent giants we see on TV documentaries, but there are sharks that can be raised in aquariums. The smaller specimens are technically "shark fish," and are more akin to minnows, but they have the trademark, streamlined look of their giant brethren.

For brackish or saltwater tank enthusiasts, small species of true sharks or *Elasmobranchii* are definitely an option. Most of these sharks are under 2 feet (0.609 meters) in length. They do require big tanks, but for people who really want to live with and study these fascinating creatures, the investment in time, money, and space is well worth it. If you are new to aquaculture, it's a good rule of thumb to decide on the focal point of your tank and make all decisions based on what that fish needs.

Sharks in the Ocean vs. Sharks in Your Tank

Remember that any aquarium seeks to recreate a natural environment for its population down to the tiniest detail. That's true of freshwater tropical aquariums with 20 gallons (75.7 liters) or less, and it's equally true of 200-gallon (757 liter) saltwater tanks with elaborate filtration and skimming systems.

If you want to raise sharks, don't treat the process as something you can just "run out and buy." You need to carefully plan each step of the ecosystem or environment you are about to create. Because a new tank must be "cycled," two months may pass before you can introduce a single fish.

Regardless, you're about to set out on a fantastic adventure that will give you a window into a world humans can only visit, but never truly inhabit.

Sharks literally breathe the water in which they swim. We are only visitors there, or, if we keep these animals as pets, hosts. The first step is not to decide what kind of tank you need, but rather what kind of shark you want to raise.

3

Not All Aquarium "Sharks" Are Sharks

By choosing the kind of shark you want to have in your tank, you immediately set in motion a path for all the other decisions you will make regarding equipment purchases, tank design, placement, and maintenance.

Let's work with a specific example using two common "starter" species of freshwater shark fish, the Bala Shark fish and the Red Tail Shark fish.

Bala Shark - Docile But Large

The Bala Shark is one of the easiest freshwater species to keep. They are one of several species of shark fish that are close relatives of the minnow. Balas are social, friendly creatures that get along well with smaller fish, especially if they've been raised together.

They like to swim and school with their own kind, or with any species that will congregate with them.

One charming thing about a Bala Shark is that they will often have a "best friend" of another species in the tank, a situation that is fascinating to watch from the other side of the glass.

A Bala Shark will grow to a maximum length of 16 inches (60.6 cm). In ideal conditions, they can reach 24 inches (61 cm), but that's rare in home aquariums. At minimum, these fish need a tank 6 feet long (1.8 meters).

(Four feet, or 1.2 meters, really isn't enough for a fish that spends its day swimming back and forth "on patrol" and that loves to school.)

The instant you decide you want a Bala, your planning process begins to involve all the factors relative to the tank that fish needs.

Start with a consideration of weight. A tank that is 6' x 2' (1.82 m x .61 m) will hold 180 gallons of water (681.37 liters) and, when fully equipped, will weigh more than 2,000 lbs. (907.18 kg)

The next item on your list immediately becomes a stand sufficient to support that weight, and then you need to think about tank placement. That means considering both matters of structural stability and weight bearing, as well as the effect of light.

Put an aquarium too close to a source of direct sunlight, and you'll be waging a constant war with algae growth.

If this is the direction you decide to go, buying the Bala Shark itself is a $3 to $12 purchase (£2 - £8). The approximate cost of the tank that fish will need to live happily (with none of the additional required equipment) is $1,350 (£860).

Red Tail Shark - Aggressive But Small

If you don't have room for a six-foot tank (1.82 m), you could opt to raise a Red Tail Shark. They are also a close relative of the minnow, and are the smallest of the freshwater shark fish.

A Red Tail rarely grows to more than 6 inches in length (15.24 cm), and can be housed in a 20-gallon (75.7 liter) tank.

An aquarium of this size can be easily purchased at a mainstream pet retail shop. Generally they are available as kits, with all equipment included, for approximately $200-$250 (£127 - £159) The Red Tail itself will be no more than $3 - $5 (£2 - £3).

You need to realize, however, that going with a Red Tail Shark, you're inviting a little bully with a Napoleon complex into your tank. Red Tails pick fights with other fish in the tank — often to the death. They exhibit extreme territoriality, and they're jumpers.

Never put a Red Tail in a tank without a lid. You'll come home and find your supremely confident, but unwittingly suicidal fish dead on the floor.

Also, <u>you can only have one Red Tail shark at a time</u>, since they are even more aggressive with others of their own kind.

Managing Tank Aggression

When you keep shark fish or true sharks, one of the greatest challenges is managing your community. Some species of sharks have to be the only one of their kind in the tank (or the only fish in the tank period.)

Never introduce a shark of any sort into an existing tank without researching its personality profile and those of the fish with which it will live. Most aggression in an aquarium is over territory. Many species, including sharks, stake out an area to call their own and will literally defend it to the death.

As a general rule of thumb, fish that exhibit territoriality are more aggressive to their own kind, which will limit the numbers of sharks you can keep.

The Red Tail shark we just discussed is a perfect example. They will get along well with other semi-aggressive fish, but not with other sharks.

It's equally important to remember that for as much as you may want to think of your tank as a peaceful, placid environment, there is still a food chain in operation.

Many species, like the Rainbow Shark, for instance, get along well with fish of their own size, but will eat smaller tank mates. Other sharks will munch happily on any invertebrates you've added to the community.

Don't lose sight of the fact that you are managing an ecosystem where the rules of nature apply even in microcosm. If you introduce predators to the environment, you can hardly expect them to be anything but what they are -- predators.

Aquarium Dividers Are Rarely an Option with Sharks

When a fish is being a bully, the best option is to segregate the aggressor. For smaller species, aquarists can divide the tank with a simple, clear partition. These are easily purchased for tanks up to 20 gallons (75.7 liters), but would have to be specially designed for larger aquariums.

With sharks, however, given their already considerable spatial needs, dividing the available space simply isn't an option in most cases. If the shark you're trying to raise has a minimum requirement for a tank 6 feet long (1.8 meters), you can't start dividing up the limited room to handle aggression.

If you truly have a desire to keep sharks and smaller, more docile fish, you'd be far better served to maintain one big shark tank and a smaller tropical tank.

It is possible, however, that when you understand the degree of work involved in keeping an aquarium large enough to accommodate sharks, managing the personal interactions of its inhabitants won't be on your list of "problems."

Chapter 2 – Keeping Sharks in a Home Aquarium

Three factors will guide your decision about keeping sharks in a home aquarium:

- Species hardiness
- Shark availability
- Shark compatibility

Hardiness refers to the ease with which a species of shark can adapt to living in captivity.

This is rarely a problem with shark fish, but can be an issue with true sharks. Many larger sharks refuse to eat when introduced to a new tank and must be enticed with special treats.

Availability refers to the ease with which a given shark can be obtained.

Shark-like fish are readily available, but some true sharks may be hard to acquire and expensive to purchase.

Tank-raised Black-Banded or Marbled Bamboo Cat Sharks sell for $60 to $70 (£38 to £45), but a Port Jackson Shark retails for $300+ (£194) depending on size.

Also known as the Horn Shark, this particular species, which reaches 5 feet in length (1.52 meters), needs a 1000 gallon (3785.4 liter) aquarium.

Compatibility is not only a reference to how the shark will get along with other fish, but also with any invertebrates in the tank.

Shark Tank by Water Type

Shark-like fish and true sharks are kept in three basic types of tanks:

1. Freshwater / tropical
2. Saltwater / marine
3. Brackish

While freshwater tanks can be quite large, most shark-like fish are not, remaining under 2 feet (61 cm) in length.

"True" or marine sharks are kept in saltwater tanks, which require a much more complex understanding of water chemistry and an extensive array of filtration and water moving equipment.

Brackish tanks are the intermediate range between the other two environments and seek to replicate spots where rivers meet the sea. In estuaries and similar points of convergence, species thrive that pass back and forth between fresh and saltwater environments.

Among aquarists, brackish tanks are considered to be the logical stepping stone between freshwater and marine tanks.

Introduction to Basic Water Chemistry

Water chemistry is a topic of endless discussion among aquarists, to the point that it almost comes across as an obsession to those not "in the know."

However, if you stop and consider that you are responsible for maintaining the liquid atmosphere your fish are breathing, the "obsession" suddenly becomes quite clear.

Without good water, your sharks will die. The longer you work with a tank, the more you will understand the necessary testing involved in maintaining optimal conditions.

As a minimal introduction to this chemistry, there are three measurements with which you should be familiar.

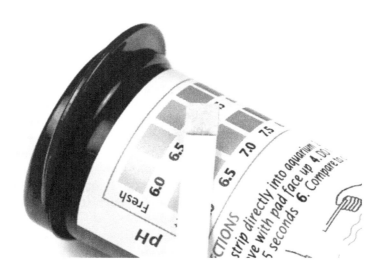

Per Hydrogen (pH)

Most people have a basic understanding of pH in relation to acidity. The lower the pH level the more acidic the water.

A higher pH means the water is basic (contains more alkaline.)

Expressed in a scale, pH 5 is slightly acidic; pH 7 is neutral; and pH 8 is basic (alkaline.)

The specific measurement is that of the balance in the water between hydrogen (H+) and hydroxide (OH) ions.

- Saltwater has a pH range of 7.5 to 8.4

- Freshwater has a pH range of 6.5 to 7.5

- Brackish water has a pH of 7.5 or greater

Carbonate Hardness (KH)

This measurement can be confusing. It is an expression of the water's alkalinity, which is not the same as "alkaline."

Alkalinity quantifies the water's ability to act as a "buffer," absorbing and neutralizing acid. The higher the KH (the greater the alkalinity of the water), the less likely it will be to experience shifts in pH level. Therefore, a higher KH level means more chemically stable water.

Specific Gravity (sg)

In a saltwater aquarium, specific gravity is the measure of relative salinity in comparison to pure water. The measurement is taken with a hydrometer or a refractometer.

The specific gravity of natural seawater varies by location in a range of 1.020 to 1.030. For a saltwater aquarium, the usual target is 1.022. It's important to establish a range and not vary from it widely.

Most creatures will adjust to any specific gravity within reason, but not to fluctuations.

Cycling Your Tank

Regardless of the type of water you are maintaining, the nitrogen cycle must be established in the tank before fish are introduced. This is not an "instant" process, and requires the cultivation of biological processes that create water with sufficient bacteria to keep marine species alive in a closed environment.

The steps in the cycle are as follows:

- Your fish produces waste materials.

- Waste materials produce ammonia in the water, which is toxic to fish.

- Ammonia feeds nitrifying bacteria present in the water.

- The bacteria eat the ammonia and produce nitrite.

- Nitrite is in turn eaten by other bacteria that produce relatively harmless nitrate.

The toxic effects of the ammonia produced by the waste materials in the water are thus cancelled out by a biological food chain.

Aquarium water is filtered and a portion of the water is changed regularly to manage nitrate levels.

The nitrogen cycle, however, preserves the chemical balance of the water. Aquarists test their tank water frequently, and monitor its quality to preserve this balance.

Depending on how this cycle is initially established, appropriately conditioning the water in your new tank may take as long as 6 to 8 weeks.

Considerations in Cycling a Saltwater Tank

To cycle your saltwater tank, there are four methods at your disposal:

- The use of chemicals
- The introduction of a source of ammonia
- The use of starter fish like damsels
- The presence of live rock

In the most simplistic sense, cycling comes down to two approaches, with or without fish.

"With fish" is the traditional way, but is not always the most preferred because the levels of nitrite and ammonia do reach toxic levels and can kill the "starter" fish.

One reason damsels are used for this purpose is because they are hardy enough to survive the process, but they will suffer considerable stress, which many see as inhumane.

The "without fish" approach requires that ammonia be introduced with dead decomposing matter or with fish waste. The resulting bacteria converts the ammonia into nitrites, which are then converted to nitrates.

The goal is to create an environment where nitrates are kept below 10 parts per million.

Note that when cycling without fish, water temperatures are raised to between 86° - 95° F (30° - 35° C) as the water is stabilized. The temperature must then be lowered back down to 74 - 80° F (23.3° - 26.6° C) slowly so as not to stress the bacteria that has just been created.

Methods for Cycling a Freshwater Tank

For freshwater tanks, cycling without fish present in the water is the preferred method. If fish are used, they would be "starter" fish that would likely die due to the high toxicity of the water during this process.

Before your community fish and any included sharks can be added to the tank, the nitrogen cycle in the water must be in place. This can take as long as four weeks.

(Note, the following material is intended as an overview of the cycling procedure. Research this process thoroughly, since you are creating a stable environment capable of supporting your tank's population. Without an intact nitrogen cycle, the water in the tank cannot support aquatic life.)

Household ammonia is acceptable to cycle a tank, as long as it is pure, with no additives present. The level in the water (which should be de-chlorinated) should be brought up to a range of 2-4 ppm.

You'll need an ammonia test kit for this purpose. Expect to test the water every 24 hours.

Next add a large handful of fish food to the water, and continuing testing at 24-hour intervals until the ammonia level begins to drop.

At this point, the ammonia is being broken down into nitrite.

Add more ammonia to bring the water back up to the target parts per million. You should now be testing for both ammonia and nitrite every 24 hours and continuing to add ammonia to the water to feed the bacteria.

When the nitrite levels begin to drop, add more ammonia.

You are looking to achieve

- 0 ppm ammonia
- 0 ppm nitrite
- A nitrate reading

The water is now ready for fish. Do a large water change (70-90%) to achieve a nitrate level of less than 40ppm.

Continue testing to monitor for spikes in ammonia and nitrites.

Brackish Aquarium Cycling and Conversion

There is little difference in cycling a brackish aquarium as opposed to a freshwater tank. The choices are still the same: with or without fish.

The real issue lies in the often transitional nature of the brackish tank.

It is quite common for an aquarist to convert a tank to a brackish environment as a first step toward keeping a saltwater aquarium.

Introducing salt to the water is a major environmental change, and cannot be done quickly.

Never increase the salinity of your water by more than .002 sg at a time. You will kill the bacteria in the water, and likely the fish in the tank.

- **Let a full month pass before you up the salinity levels again.**

Do not attempt to convert a freshwater tank to brackish water without fully researching the water chemistry involved and understanding the potential effects on the existing population.

Undoubtedly your goal in converting your tank is to acquire new fish species, including sharks, but understand you will likely need to relocate some of the fish you already own that cannot tolerate higher salt content in the water.

Basic Tank Cleaning and Maintenance

Try to think of your aquarium as a smoothly functioning system. Each day, as you feed the fish, or simply watch their interactions, take the time to evaluate how each component of the system is functioning.

Look and Listen

Immediately assess anything that does not sound or look right. Over time, you will become familiar with the noises your equipment makes. If a filter starts producing a strange sound, don't just let it go. Find out why.

Failure to maintain correct water quality is the number one cause of death in aquarium fish.

Watch

How are your fish behaving? Are they eating? Do they look healthy? Are they exhibiting any unusual behavior?

If you see anything that doesn't seem right, perform a water test and examine the individuals closely for any sign of disease, which often manifests with spots, diminished coloration, fungal growth, or even rot.

Make a Schedule

In addition to constantly monitoring water quality, create a routine for:

- Partial water changes
- Gravel vacuuming
- Filter servicing
- Algae removal
- Comprehensive water testing

Computerized tank monitoring is extremely helpful in keeping up with these tasks, but it does not take the place of the actual manual labor involved. That's up to you.

Water Changes and Gravel Vacuuming

Although the frequency of water changes will vary by tank configuration, consider the following broad guidelines:

- 25% water change every two weeks

- Include a partial vacuuming of the gravel to remove debris in the procedure.

- When you change the water unplug the heaters, powerheads, power filters, and power pumps. Also remove ornamentation to facilitate gravel cleaning. Don't forget to agitate the substrate to loosen embedded debris.

- Depending on the type of vacuum you purchase and the power capacity relative to the size of your tank, expect to pay $50-$100 (£32-£65).

- Always make sure the water you are putting in is the *same temperature* as the existing tank water and has been dechlorinated and subject to any other required treatments, including the addition of marine salt if you are working with a saltwater aquarium.

(Note that pre-mixed saltwater should be aerated and agitated for 24 hours prior to addition to the tank to ensure the correct SG has been achieved.)

- If necessary, scrape and remove any algae growing on the sides of the tank.

- Always be sensitive to the amount of nitrifying bacteria you are removing during water changes. It is imperative to maintain the nitrogen cycle in your tank.

(*Please note that there are many, many products and tools available to assist with maintaining aquariums. Apply the same level of research to selecting this equipment. Successful tanks are dependent on good water quality, which is the goal of regular and thorough maintenance.*)

Dietary Considerations for Sharks

True sharks will not thrive on a diet of pure protein like shrimp or smaller fish. Expect to supplement your shark's diet with tablets or gels that provide essential vitamins and minerals.

Mazuri, a company specializing in exotic pet foods, makes a line of shark and ray dietary supplement products. See http://www.mazuri.com

As an example, 2 lbs. (.9 kg) of the Mazuri product Vita-Zu Shark/Ray Tablets provides water and fat soluble vitamins and minerals and helps to decrease the risk of iodine deficiency. It retails for $110 (£71).

Sharks that do not receive adequate nutrition develop wasting diseases. They may be subject to goiter from a lack of iodine, or suffer from spinal twisting due to a lack of Vitamin C and Vitamin A.

In researching the type of shark you plan to keep, it is vital to look into the animal's specific dietary requirements, including feeding habits.

The Bamboo Shark, for instance, is both nocturnal and benthic (bottom dwelling).

The Leopard Shark is semi-pelagic, meaning that in nature it inhabits the upper layers of the open sea.

Is There an Ideal Shark for the Home Aquarium?

"Ideal" is a relative term. What you can afford in terms of tank space, time, and commitment to shark husbandry is ideal for your situation, but might prove impossible for another aquarist.

That being said, if you can make a choice within these parameters, your chances of *successfully* keeping true sharks in a home tank go up considerably.

- A tank of 180 to 500 gallons. (681.37 to 1892.7 liters)

- The selection of a small, docile shark that adapts well to captivity and will eat.

- A shark that puts on a satisfying presentation in the tank.

Remember that tank size is always the dominant consideration. Experts say that a good rule of thumb is to take the maximum adult length of the shark in which you are interested and multiply it by 3 to get the minimum tank length.

A two-foot shark x 3 = 6 foot tank (.609 meters / 1.83 meters)

In "Sharks for the Aquarium and Consideration for Their Selection," published in 2010 by the Florida Cooperative Extension Service, Institute of Food and Agricultural Sciences at the University of Florida, authors Alexis L. Morris, Elisa J. Livengood, and Frank A. Chapman picked five true sharks as "ideal" for marine hobbyists. They were:

1. Bamboo Shark (white spotted and brown banded), at a length of 3.4 ft (104 cm)

2. Coral Catshark, at a length of 2.3 ft (70 cm)

3. Horn Shark, at a length of 4 ft (120 cm)

4. Leopard Shark at a length of 4.9 ft (150cm)

5. Port Jackson Shark, at a length of 4.4 ft (137 cm)

But remember, keeping sharks is a game of numbers. If you want a 5-foot Leopard Shark (1.52 meters), you will technically need a 15-foot (4.57 meter) aquarium or basically a swimming pool.

When this question was put to enthusiasts on Yahoo Answers in 2011, a master aquarist offered these specifications for a home Leopard Shark tank.

- 12' long (3.65 meters)
- 12' wide (3.65 meters)
- 4' deep (1.21 meters)
- 4,208.8 gallons (at 8 lbs per gallon 33,670.4 lbs. or 16.8 tons / 15.24 metric tonnes)

Conservatively, the tank alone would cost $15,000 / £9725.

Thankfully, there are other options that will still satisfy the enthusiast's desire to keep sharks.

Buying Sharks Online

Buying live animals online is a highly controversial business at best. The greatest issue with sharks is simply transporting an animal that requires a liquid environment to survive and that is highly susceptible to stress.

Fully Consider Site Language and Policies

One site that stands out, www.SharkSupply.com openly addresses such issues. For instance, on a listing for Hammerhead Shark pups, the site says:

"DO NOT CALL us if you do not have a 20-30 foot system for this species!!! Also, if you do not have several thousand dollars just for the truck shipment cost, please, do not waste our time. Few shark keepers can house a hammerhead."

This site also includes a conservation policy written by the business owner, which reads in part:

"As I advertise on this web site, my aim has always been to have an environmental footprint that is nearly invisible. I can say with confidence that in almost 15 years of working with sharks, I have not negatively impacted the shark populations at all. I have done more than my part in promoting and maintaining our aquatic resources. I plan in the future to continue in this policy of resource responsibility. Regardless of how large our sales may grow, the overarching concern is the minimizing of our impact on the environment. I hope to continue in the forefront of ideas and experimentation in promoting population friendly solutions to the demands of our industry."

(The complete policy can be found at:
http://sharksupply.com/conserve_policy.htm)

Certainly this is not the only site online selling live sharks,
but it is an example of the kinds of things to look for in
considering an online supplier.

**A strong emphasis on ethics and a concern for the health
of the animals should be prominent in the site language.**

In this instance, the company requires photographic or
other proof of tank size for an order to be placed. This is an
excellent practice, and emblematic of someone who cares
about the animals they are selling.

Do Your Research Outside a Commercial Site

At the same time, however, do not accept site language on
face value alone. Go to a discussion forum like
MonsterFishKeepers.com and see if there is any mention of
the commercial site you are considering.

In a discussion thread from 2006, SharkSupply.com's assertion of "mini" bull sharks for sale is debated among members.

(See http://www.monsterfishkeepers.com/forums/showthread.php?37737-Mini-Bull-Sharks. Note, this is a public discussion forum and off color language is used.)

Bull Sharks reach a maximum length of 5'-6' (1.524-1.828 meters), so the claim of a "mini" version of this massive fish is greeted with considerable derision by the forum members.

In the discussion, however, the actual identity of the shark in question is nailed down as the Finetooth, a shark that does average 5' (1.524 meters) in length, and is indigenous to the southeastern and gulf coasts of the United States.

As the discussion continues, the members thoroughly pick apart the site, a thread which provides a good basis of evaluation for potential customers.

To Buy of Not to Buy Online

In the end, only you can decide. There are many factors that will color your decision, including, but not limited to:

- Purchase price.
- Shipping costs.
- Transit time.
- Sensitivity of the species in question.

Your paramount concern should always be the welfare of the shark. If you have any reservations, arrange to acquire your shark by a different method of delivery.

Chapter 3 - Freshwater Shark Tanks

There are many freshwater "shark-like" fish that can be kept in 50 gallon (189.27 liters) to 70 gallon (264.97 liters) tanks.

Tanks of this size are easier to set up because they can be purchased as complete "kits" that come with all the essential equipment.

A 50-gallon (189.27 liter) rectangular acrylic aquarium sold as a complete package costs about $500 (£318).

(It's actually a good idea for a beginning aquarist to have a large tank because it's easier to maintain proper water quality.)

Equipment for a Freshwater Tank

When you purchase a freshwater kit, or buy the pieces individually, you will need:

> ➤ **A filtration system, either an "under gravel" filter or a power filter mounted on the back of the tank.**

If you go with an "under gravel" system, you will want to make sure the air pump and powerhead are large enough for the volume of water in the tank.

If you opt for a power filter, make sure it is large enough to circulate the volume of water at a rate of 5 gallons per hour or approximately 18.93 liters per hour. Thus a 50 gallon / 189.27 liter tank would need a filter rated for 250 gallons / 946.35 liters per hour.

> ➤ **A heater, which should be fully submersible for ease of use.**

You should use a heater with an adjustable thermostat. In terms of wattage, you'll want 3-5 watts per gallon of water, so a 50 gallon (189.27 liter) tank would require a 150-250 watt heater. Although it varies by species, most fish like water between 70-80° F (21.1-26.6 C).

> ➤ **Sand or gravel substrate sufficient to lay down 2 to 3 inches (7.62 cm) in the bottom of the tank.**

Always make sure the substrate matches the needs of your fish. Some sharks are bottom dwellers with sensitive bellies. The kit will also include a lighting system, possibly a hood (some fish are jumpers), and decorative items like plastic plants and structures suitable for fish to use as hiding places.

Tank Placement

You will not only need adequate floor space for your tank, but you want to avoid an area with too much sunlight as this will promote excessive algae growth, which means a high level of maintenance for you.

Try to find an interior wall away from bright light.

Also, consider the weight bearing capacity of the area.

- 50 gallons (189.27 liters) of water weighs 400 lbs. (181.43 kg)

- 70 gallons (264.97 liters) of water weighs 560 lbs. (254 kg)

You will need an electrical outlet nearby, and you will be hauling water for weekly maintenance. Keep all these factors in mind.

Check for Leaks and Fill the Tank

Rinse the gravel thoroughly with running water in a colander before creating the "floor" of your aquarium. You can also add all decorative items and plants (real or artificial) at this time.

(If you are using an "under gravel" filtration system, it will be laid down first, and the gravel placed on top of the equipment as per the instructions.)

Next, fill the tank with about two inches of water (5.08 cm) and let it sit for half an hour. If there are any leaks, they should show up in that amount of time.

Always try to catch leaks before you fill the aquarium completely. There won't be an enormous mess, and it's better to return the tank to the store before you've done too much with it.

When you have determined that there are no leaks, fill the tank to a height of 1 inch (2.54 cm) under the rim. If you are using an external power filter, set it up at this time.
Let the tank run for 24 hours, monitoring the functioning of the equipment, and continue to look for any sign of leaking.

Managing the Tank Population

Once the fish are added, manage the population by size and temperament. Smaller shark-like fish do best with fish of their own size.

Many species are aggressive, and can only be the sole "shark" in the tank. Others like to school, and will co-exist happily in the community.

Chapter 3 - Freshwater Shark Tanks

Shark Profiles: Freshwater

Bala Shark

Also known as the "Silver Shark," these shark fish have a semi-aggressive temperament and take a moderate level of care. They reach a maximum size of 1'4" (40.64 cm) and require, at minimum a 70 gallon (264.97 liter) aquarium.

Bala Sharks are omnivores, and are found in black, white, and yellow colorations.

They are active and visible during the day, with striking silver metallic bodies, and black dorsal and caudal fins. Bala Sharks are relatively passive.

Bala sharks need dense vegetation, driftwood, and rocks. They do best in groups of 3 or more, and like to school.

Flaked food, vegetable-based foods, and freeze-dried bloodworms are good food choices for this species.

> ➢ Ideal water conditions: 72-79° F , (22.2 – 26.11° C) KH 10-15, pH 6.5-7.5

Redtail Shark

The Redtail Shark Fish (also known as the White Tipped Shark) is a semi-aggressive omnivore, requiring moderate care, and at least a 50 gallon (189.27 liter) tank.

These beautiful fish have a stunning black body with a bright red tail and a white-tipped dorsal fin. Typically they reach a maximum length of 4" (10.16 cm).

Redtail Sharks do best as the sole sharks in a tank with fish of a similar size. They are fairly territorial, and like dense vegetation, and features like driftwood and rocks.

Appropriate feeds include freeze-dried bloodworms, vegetable-based foods, and flake food.

> ➢ Ideal water conditions: 72-79° F (22.2 – 26.11° C), KH 10-15, pH 6.5-7.5

Siamese Algae Eater

Siamese Algae Eaters are peaceful fish requiring only moderate care. They do very well in tanks of 30 gallons (113.56 liters) or more, but they do like planted aquariums with lots of plants with broad leaves for resting.

In addition to eating algae in the tank, they require a typical diet of flaked and pelleted foods and freeze-dried bloodworms.

At purchase, your Siamese Algae Eater will be 1.25" to 1.5" (3.175 – 3.81 cm) in length, and it will not grow larger than 6" (15.24 cm).

> ➢ Ideal water conditions: 75-79° F (23.88 – 26.11° C), KH 5-10, pH 6.5-7.0

Columbian Shark

The Columbian Shark (or Black Fin Shark) is a peaceful catfish with long "whiskers." They are easy to care for and peaceful by nature, but are best suited for 70 gallon (264.97 liter) tanks and larger as they can reach a maximum size of 10" (25.4 cm).

> ➤ Ideal water conditions: 74-79° F (23.3 – 26.11° C), KH 10-12, pH 7.0-7.5

These fish like an environment with plenty of plants and rocks. They will eat smaller tank mates, and can survive in fresh and saltwater. (They do quite well in brackish tanks.)

Appropriate foods include high-quality algae, bloodworms, and catfish pellets.

Black Shark

The Black Shark (or Black Labeo) reaches a maximum size of 2' (0.60 meters) and need a tank of 70 gallons (264.97 liters) or more. They are aggressive fish requiring moderate care. They do not do well in community tanks and should not be kept in planted aquariums since they will eat the plants. Because Black Sharks are jumpers, always use a hood on the tank.

> ➤ Ideal water conditions: 75-81° F (23.88 – 27.22° C), KH 10-15, pH 6.5-7.5

Feed Black Sharks vegetable-based foods, freeze-dried bloodworms, and flake food.

Albino Rainbow Shark

Also called the Albino Ruby Shark, Albino Red-Finned Shark, and Iridescent Shark, this fish is semi-aggressive. They are best kept as solo sharks with fish of a similar size.

With an overall pink coloration and bright red fins, they make a beautiful addition to an aquarium.

> ➢ Ideal water conditions: 72-79° F (22.22 – 26.11° C), KH 10-15, pH 6.5-7.5

Keep an Albino Rainbow Shark in a tank with spots of dense vegetation, rocks, and driftwood to accommodate their territorial nature.

Good food choices are flaked, vegetable-based foods and freeze-dried bloodworms.

Chinese Hi Fin Banded Shark

Also known as the Chinese or Sailfin Sucker, Asian Sucker, and Entsuyui, this fish has no teeth in its mouth, but does have a row of teeth forming a comb in its throat.

When kept in a tank, they routinely reach a length of 18" (45.72 cm), so they need at least 125 gallons (473.17 liters) and are best suited for aquarists comfortable with advanced tank management. Well-oxygenated water is a must for this species, as is good water flow.

They are peaceful, and do well as algae eaters in garden ponds, tolerating temperatures as low as 40° F (4.44° C).

> ➢ Ideal water conditions: 59-82° F, (15 – 27.77° C) KH 4-20, pH 6.5-7.5

Essentially an herbivore, this fish lives on bottom-dwelling invertebrates and algae, but will also eat freeze-dried or frozen bloodworms.

Silver Apollo Shark

An active fish that loves to school, the Silver Apollo Shark is relatively passive, but does best in a well-established, planted aquarium of 30 gallons (113.56 liters) or more. They do tend to be jumpers, so expect to use a hood.

> ➤ Ideal water conditions: 68-77° F (20 - 25° C), KH 5-8, pH 6.0-6.5

These fish take a very standard diet of flaked and pelleted vegetable based foods and freeze-dried bloodworms.

Rainbow Shark

The Rainbow Shark (Ruby Shark or Red-Finned Shark) grows to a maximum length of 6"(15.24 cm). They are semi-aggressive and should be the only shark in a tank with fish of an equal size.
Rainbow Sharks are beautiful, with red fins against a dark gray to blackish body, but they will eat smaller fish and are territorial, wanting rocks and dense vegetation in a tank of at least 50 gallons (189.27 liters).

> ➤ Ideal water conditions: 72-79° F (22.22 – 26.11° C), KH 10-15, pH 6.5-7.5

They have no special dietary needs, and do quite well on flaked vegetable foods.

Rose Line Shark

Alternate names for this fish include Denison Barb and Red Lined Torpedo Barb. They are long fish, but not especially large, reaching only 4.5" (11.43 cm).

They are silver with a black line down their bodies. A red stripe runs over the eye to a point just under the dorsal fin, which has a red leading edge and yellow and black accents.

This peaceful fish does very well in a large community aquarium. They are jumpers, and prefer to be kept in groups. A tank of at least 50 gallons (189.27 liters) with a high oxygen level is best for this species.

> ➢ Ideal water conditions: 60-77° F (15.55 - 25° C), KH 4-10, pH 6.8-7.8

Rose Line Sharks will eat both meaty and vegetable foods with brine shrimp and bloodworms for variety.

Chapter 4 – Saltwater Shark Tanks

Saltwater aquariums involve a solid understanding of water chemistry in order to maintain stable conditions. Without the correct equipment and proper maintenance, your fish will not survive.

The following material is intended as an <u>introductory overview</u> of these factors, as well as the basic installation steps. The text is not meant to be a comprehensive, all-inclusive list or set of instructions, but rather an introduction to initiate more detailed research.

Determining Tank Size and Weight

The minimum tank size recommended to keep true shark species is 6' x 2' (1.82 m x .61 m), a volume sufficient to contain 180 gallons of water (681.37 liters).

A more ideal arrangement would be a tank 8' x 4' x 2' (2.43m x 1.21m x 0.60m), which would hold 480 gallons (1,817 liters).

It is extremely important to calculate the weight of any tank you are contemplating designing. A single gallon of water weighs 8 lbs. (3.63 kg), therefore:

- 180 gallons of water weighs 1,440 lbs. (653.17 kg)

- 480 gallons of water weighs 3,840 lbs. (1741.8 kg)

Do not skimp on the stand for your tank, or on the foundation on which it will sit. Chances are very good that a tank large enough to hold a shark cannot be placed on the second floor of a structure.

Even when placed on the ground level, unless the unit is sitting directly on a concrete slab, the floor under it may need to be reinforced.

Expect to dedicate about 12-26 sq. ft. of floor space for your shark tank. $(1.11m^2 - 2.41m^2)$.

Essential Equipment for a Saltwater Shark Tank

Aquascaping, the art of creating a lifelike and authentic underwater environment in a tank, is an art form. Underlying that art, however, are some very necessary mechanics.

You will need to learn about every one of these pieces of equipment in detail, and how they interact with one another to create a fully functioning saltwater environment in which marine sharks can live.

> ➤ One point, however, cannot be emphasized strongly enough **you cannot just fill a tank with salt water and put some sharks in it.**

> ➤ Your tank must be fully designed and functioning, and must have the appropriate water chemistry in place to sustain marine life long before any sharks are introduced to the water. ***This can take up to two months.***

In that period, you'll be looking at an empty, bubbling aquarium. This is, however, your opportunity to learn everything there is to learn about your tank and about the fish that will call it home.

Any time you are setting up a shark aquarium, *moving slowly and deliberately* to get each step of the process right is your best option.

Protein Skimmer

A protein skimmer creates tiny bubbles inside a reaction chamber. Waste materials become attached to the bubbles, which rise to the surface, carrying the waste with them. There, they are removed into a collection cup that will be emptied daily.

The bubbles also serve to replenish oxygen throughout the tank, which in turn helps maintain a stable pH level. (At night, carbon dioxide can build up in the water and lower the pH.)

Always buy the largest skimmer you can afford. The bigger the unit, the more efficiently it will operate, and the easier the tank will be to maintain.

Expect to pay approximately $350 (£223) for a protein skimmer sufficient for a 180 gallon (681.37 liter) tank.

Note: Equipment prices vary widely. All estimates included in this text are for mid-range, high quality units and are meant as "ballpark" numbers only. Creating a viable saltwater environment involves a great deal of research, both into your livestock and into the equipment that will support their habitat.

Pumps/Powerheads

Pumps or powerheads circulate water inside the tank. Your goal is to "turn over" the water anywhere from 6 to 10 times per hour.

Again, some of this calculation of "flow rate" is dependent on the type of shark you are raising. Bottom dwellers, for instance, are not going to like sitting in a moving current.

The equipment will come with a GPH or (gallons per hour) or LPH (Liters per hour) rating. You must consider, however, any elements that create resistance to that flow.

You want good water movement, especially as water will need to be lifted back through the sump and into the tank. Consequently, it's better to err slightly on the higher side of water moving capacity.

Depending on the number of powerheads your tank will require, costs for water moving equipment for a 180 gallon (681.37 liter) could range from $100 to $500 (£64 to £319).

Note: If you are new to aquaculture, you may not fully understand the "culture" part of that word. People who keep high-level tanks can and do talk endlessly about the equipment and equations involved. It's a very good idea to make friends with more experienced and seasoned saltwater aquarists. The Internet has made it possible to connect with enthusiasts around the world who are knowledgeable in keeping all kinds of fish.

Salt

Salt for use in aquariums is an ongoing expense. As a rough estimate, 5 gallons (18.92 liters) of salt is sufficient to produce about 150 gallons (567.81 liters) of saltwater, at a cost of roughly $50 to $75 (£32 - £48)

Reverse Osmosis De-Ionization (RODI System)

An RODI system purifies the water that will be used in your saltwater tank. It is far superior and more reliable than chemical de-chlorinating products.

These systems don't just neutralize chlorine in tap water, but also take care of other impurities like nitrates and phosphates that enter the system through plant fertilizers.

If these materials are not removed from the water, you are essentially feeding algae growth every time the tank is topped off or the water is changed out.

Since the lights used in marine tanks are very bright, aquarists have to be careful about the amount of nutrients added to the water to prevent algae growth from getting out of hand. It's much easier to prevent algae in the first place than to get rid of it after the fact.

Drinking water can actually be contaminated with everything from petrochemicals to trace pharmaceuticals. What might be considered safe for human consumption can easily kill sensitive fish like sharks and the coral and invertebrates inhabiting the tank with them.

An RODI tank gives the aquarist peace of mind that they are using the best water they can create.

The system consists of five progressive filtration steps:

1. The sediment filter removes large chunks of impurities like dirt or rust.

2. Two carbon blocks then take out the chlorine and reduce the soluble and voluble organic compounds.

3. The RO membrane removes 96%-98% of the total dissolved solids. In this phase, the water molecules pass through the membrane, which rejects larger impurities and sends them down the waste water line.

4. Water passes through the DI cartridge, which is filled with tiny beads of positively and negatively charged ions.

5. This last stage results in 0 TDS water (total dissolved solids.)

Impurities in water have a detectable electrical charge. A TDS meter reads that electrical conductivity, which returns a purity rating.

An RODI set-up for a 180 gallon (681.37 liter) tank will range from $150 to $250 (£95 to £160).

Lights

Any standard saltwater bulb will work well with a shark tank. The desired "blue" effect can be created with 50/50 style bulbs with a 10k element and an actinic element.

Newer LED lights will last longer, however, and are more energy efficient. They also create a pleasant shimmering effect in the water.

Since lighting is a major aesthetic element of aquaculture, costs can be surprisingly high to achieve the right "look." Expect a price range of $250 to $500 (£159 to £318).

Sand/Rock

Obviously live rock is not, itself, living. It is, however, inhabited by micro and macroscopic marine organisms. This element of a saltwater tank may be composed of:

- **Coral or coral rock:** Pieces of actual coral or coral rock that has broken off the outside of a reef and are encrusted with organisms including such things as sponges and coralline algae.

- **Inshore rock:** Taken from inside a reef and densely covered in such things as mussels, clams, shrimp, crab, and macroalgae.

- **Dead base rock:** Rock that is devoid of external life that can be used as a foundation on which to place living rock.

The most likely combination is a layer of dead base rock topped with coral or "reef rock," which will, in turn, seed the dead rock over time.

Live rock is the principle means of biological nitrification or filtering in your tank, and is a major aesthetic enhancement to create the natural look of the sea bottom.

The sand, which will coat the bottom of the tank, further augments the natural look and plays a minor role in filtration. Most tanks incorporate .25 to 4.0 inches (.63 to 10.16 cm) of sand.

For 25 lbs. (11.33 kg) of live rock, expect to pay $75 to $100 (£47 to £63).

> ➢ Note that some shark species are not appropriate for a reef tank because they can seriously injure their sensitive bellies on the rock.

Heater/Chiller

Proper temperature in a saltwater tank must be maintained at all times.

Depending on the placement of the tank in your home or business, the climate control systems in the building, and the climate of the region itself, you may need both a heater and a chiller.

> ➢ Note that insulating the tank can significantly improve temperature control and save on electricity since both heaters and chillers use a lot of power.

Obviously the choice, size, and combination of this kind of equipment varies widely. Heaters that can handle the needs of a 180 gallon (681.37 liter) tank average around $200 (£127), while a chiller will cost around $500 (£319).

Saltwater fish — especially sharks — are highly sensitive to temperature changes. Do not scrimp on heating and cooling equipment. Maintaining stable temperature is essential.

> ➢ The greater the amount of water, the more heat it will maintain. Think of it this way. A cup of coffee gets cold faster than a bathtub full of hot water. Therefore, aquarium chillers have to work harder than heaters.

Water Monitoring and Testing Equipment

Water monitoring and testing is a regular and vital aspect of keeping a saltwater aquarium.

The principle device to test and maintain salinity is a refractometer. A good quality unit that will return reliable measurements costs about $150 (£95).

Testing kits for various chemical levels including (but not limited to) ammonia, phosphates, and nitrites retail for $20 to $40 each (£13 to £25)

> ➢ Note that this is an ongoing, repeat expense since proper water quality is a huge part of maintaining a successful and healthy tank.

Computer Based Tank Control

Increasingly aquarists are turning to computer-based monitoring systems that measure all tank parameters via a network of sensors and probes.

This approach allows for highly specific tank management, with trends and benchmarks recorded over time.

If you can afford a set-up of this nature, you will save yourself a great deal of time and effort, and you will likely be able to spot and correct problems at their earliest appearance.

These systems handle:

- pH control
- Temperature control
- Salinity
- Water level
- Water flow

. . . and a host of other factors. Most are expandable, and can be monitored remotely over the Internet and via smartphone interfaces.

To begin your research into this level of sophistication, consider looking at the ReefKeeper series of aquarium controllers at http://www.DigitalAquatics.com

Prices vary widely depending on the degree of sophistication you plan to incorporate and on the extent to which you can use equipment you already own (computer, smartphone, Internet connection, and so on.)

If you are interested in this route, budget $500 to $1000 (£319 to £638).

Sump

The sump is a secondary tank. It's set up and linked to the main or "display" tank for the purpose of holding pre-conditioned water capable of sustaining marine life.

Not all aquarists use a sump, but it does increase total water volume and can make for a healthier tank by increasing water flow and assisting with filtration.

(It's very common for the area around the sump to be turned into a "hidden" place to store all the tank management equipment.)

A sump capable of handling 250 gallons (946.35 liters) of water costs approximately $280 (£180).

Auto Top Off System

Auto top off systems maintain the water level in the tank by refilling the aquarium with fresh water when a predetermined drop level has been reached. (Fresh water is used to maintain appropriate salinity.)

In its most basic design, a float lowers and engages the pump when a trigger point has been reached. Then when the correct water level has been once again reached, the pump shuts off.

Expect to pay approximately $175 (£112).

Backup Generator

Installing a back-up generator that will engage automatically in the event of a power failure is absolutely optional. If you take into consideration the time, effort, and expense of all the other equipment, however, plus the effort to condition the tank, not to mention the lives of the fish, the additional cost may well be worth it.

For a 7500 watt stand-by generator, expect to pay $700 to $1000 (£4467 - £638).

Overflow Box

In addition to these components, some aquarists also choose to use an overflow box for obvious reasons.

If something goes wrong with the pumping components of tanks of this size, the water damage to a home can be considerable.

Most overflow boxes retail for around $150 (£96).

Order of Installing Tank Components

Although there are certainly no "rules" for setting up a saltwater tank, the following items are the major steps to be taken, in more or less the "correct" order:

1. Purchase the tank.

2. Install an appropriate stand or foundation

3. Connect the RODI system.

4. Install the sump system.

5. Mount the skimmer, heater, chiller, and auto top off system.

6. Put sand substrate in the bottom of the tank.

7. Add rock, if applicable

8. Mount the powerheads.

9. Fill the tank with premixed saltwater.

You are NOT, however, ready to introduce fish at this point. The water must first be conditioned to become a viable marine environment.

Shark Profiles: Saltwater

Marine or saltwater sharks are considerably larger than freshwater, salt-like fish. They require more intricately balanced saltwater tanks that are significantly larger.

These creatures are, on a whole, not easy to keep and should be attempted by experienced aquarists only.

Black Banded Cat Shark

A Black Banded Cat Shark will reach a maximum length of 3'6" (1.06 meters) and requires a minimum tank size of 180 gallons (681.37 liters).

This aggressive fish should be kept by expert aquarists only.

It is a handsome carnivore with a cream body marked with black, broad stripes. Muted stripes may be present between the stripes as the fish matures, and the mouth has barbels or "whiskers."

The Cat Shark is a bottom dweller that will eat any crustacean present in the tank. Since its abdomen is easily scratched, it needs sand at the bottom of the tank.

Never expose a Cat Shark to any medication containing copper. When first introduced to an aquarium, a Cat Shark may refuse to eat and will need to be enticed with pieces of squid or live saltwater feeder shrimp.

Once its diet is established, a Cat Shark will eat shrimp, scallops, and fresh pieces of marine fish species.

> ➤ Ideal water conditions: 72-78° F (22.22 – 25.55° C), KH 8-12, pH 8.1-8.4, sg 1.020-1.025

Horn Shark

The Horn Shark, also known as the Port Jackson or Bullhead Shark is a peaceful creature indigenous to the intertidal waters around Australia.

They are suitable for expert aquarists only, reaching a maximum length of 5 feet (1.52 meters), and needing as much as 1000 gallons (3785.41 liters) of water to thrive.

They are difficult to acclimate, and may refuse to eat when first introduced to an aquarium. They must be tempted with squid or feeder shrimp in the beginning. These nocturnal feeders will prey on smaller sleeping fish.

The Horn Shark is olive green with darker green or black markings in irregular patterns. They require sand for a substrate due to the sensitive nature of their abdomen, which can be susceptible to infections. This shark should never be exposed to copper.

> ➤ Ideal water conditions: 57-70° F, KH 8-12, pH 8.1-8.4, sg 1.020-1.025

Wobbygong Shark

The aggressive Wobbygong Shark (Wobby, Wobbegong, or Wobbygone) is an aggressive green and tan shark that reaches a maximum length of 4' (1.21 meters) and requires a 300-gallon (1,135.62 liter) tank.

A bottom dweller with a flattened appearance, it features a mottled body and a "frilled" mouth.

Due to the sensitivity of the Wobbygong's belly, it needs a fine sand substrate. A finicky eater, it has the typical copper toxicity sensitivity of most sharks of this size and type.

> ➢ Ideal water conditions: 72-78° F (13.88 – 25.55 ° C), KH 8-12, pH 8.1-8.4, sg 1.020-1.025

Epaulette Shark

A relatively small bottom dweller, the Epaulette Shark reaches a maximum length of 3' 6" (1.066 meters) and needs around 360 gallons (1362.75 liters) of water.

It is an aggressive yellow and tan shark suitable for expert fish keepers only.

Like most benthic fish, the Epaulette shark needs a soft sand substrate.

It exhibits the typical reluctance to feed when introduced to a tank, and is sensitive to copper.

> ➢ Ideal water conditions: 72-78° F (22.22 – 25.55° C), KH 8-12, pH 8.1-8.4, sg 1.020-1.025

Chapter 5 - Brackish Shark Tanks

In nature, a brackish environment occurs where freshwater and saltwater meet. A brackish aquarium is set up in much the same way as the freshwater and saltwater tanks.

Since a freshwater tank is easily converted to a brackish one with the addition of marine salt and equipment like a protein skimmer, keeping a brackish tank is often a transitional project for a hobbyist.

By definition, a brackish environment is highly variable. Lagoons, coastal streams, mangrove swamps, and estuaries change with the rise and fall of the tides.

Their chemistry is affected by the amount of rainfall they receive, by the temperature in the region, and by the degree of evaporation to which they are subject.

It's very difficult to arrive at a single definition for brackish water, but there are three brackish habitats or biotopes:

1. Estuary
2. River
3. Mangrove/swamp

Species that live in these environments are classed as:

- Low salinity
- Medium salinity
- High salinity

But even these distinctions are not necessarily fixed, with most of the species showing a tolerance for change and a high level of adaptability. Generally speaking, however:

- Low salinity species live in water with 1.002 to 1.005 sg.
- Medium salinity species inhabit 1.008 to 1.025 sg (full seawater).
- High salinity species live at full seawater strength and will not thrive below 1.012 sg.

The Estuary

This is the most commonly replicated biotype for an aquarium.

Estuaries have a higher, more constant salinity than other brackish environments because in nature they lie at the mouths of large rivers in close proximity to the ocean. Tanks balanced to follow this model are easier to maintain. They require only slow to moderate water flow and good aeration to keep the pH and specific gravity levels within the correct parameters.

An additional advantage to the aquarist interested in keeping sharks is that the minimum recommended size for an estuary-based brackish tank is 55 gallons (208.19 liters).

➢ This is an ideal environment for the Columbian Shark Catfish profiled at the end of this chapter.

Specific goals for an estuary tank are:

- 78-84° F (25.5-28.8° C)
- pH 7.6 - 8.5
- Salinity 1.010 to 1.025

Rocks and clean driftwood with good branching provide perfect decorative elements and hiding places for tank inhabitants.

The Brackish River

Specific gravity is usually not as high in a brackish river, nor is it as stable. Brackish rivers tend to be highly oxygenated because they are fast flowing, with heavy plant growth on the sides of the channel.

In a tank setting, a powerhead will be necessary to move the water, and sufficient aeration is required to keep pH and SG levels within good norms.

For some aquarists, this is an ideal trial run of a brackish set-up because it can be achieved in tanks as small as 10 gallons (37.85 liters) and up to 75 gallons (283.9 liters).

In these tanks you are attempting to achieve:

- 78-84° F (25.5-28.8° C)
- pH 7.6 - 8.5
- Salinity 1.005 to 1.010

Expect to use heavy planting on the sides and of the water, with driftwood and rocks on the bottom.

Mangrove Swamp

Located along the sides of estuaries and rivers, mangrove swamps have low water levels and little movement, resulting in a mid to high range salinity level.

Most mangrove tanks are 20 gallons (75.7 liters) or larger.

In addition to fish, crabs and mud skippers are often present.

These tanks tend to be long and shallow, rather than tall and deep.

The mangroves themselves, which are excellent to export nutrients, can be used as the main filter in these tanks.

Specific parameters to achieve are:

- 78-84° F (25.5-28.8° C)
- pH 7.8 - 8.5
- Salinity 1.010 to 1.015

You will need mangroves, floating plants, rocks, and driftwood or bogwood on the bottom.

Required Equipment

Beyond the tank itself, you will need typical freshwater aquarium equipment including:

➤ Filters sufficient to turn the water 10 times per hour at minimum.

➤ A heater rated for both fresh and saltwater use.

➤ Plants that will grow in saltwater and appropriate for the biotope you are creating.

➤ Substrate, typically something sandy for this type tank.

➤ Marine salt.

➤ Test kits that handle both fresh and saltwater tests.*

* You will need to perform pH and KH tests with a saltwater kit, and all other tests with a freshwater kit.

Mixing Brackish Water

In mixing water for a brackish tank:

- 1.025 sg water contains about 4.7 ounces of marine salt per gallon

- 1.010 sg water contains about 2.0 ounces of marine salt per gallon

One of the keys to achieving a brackish state in a tank is to mix the water in a bucket and arriving at the desired salinity before adding it to the tank. Remember, you can add more salt, but you can't take salt out of the water once it's mixed.

The good news, however, is that brackish fish don't require exact salinity. It is this very tolerance for a margin of error that attracts many people to brackish aquaculture, especially those that are daunted by the demands of a full saltwater tank.

Populating Your Brackish Tank

After your tank has been appropriately cycled, you will need to select species in keeping with the level of salinity you are maintaining:

- Low salinity species include fish like the Orange and Green Chromides, Pike Livebearers, Knight Gobies, and Figure-8 Pufferfish.

- Medium salinity fish include scats, violet gobies, some archerfish, monos, and the Colombian Shark Catfish

- High salinity species include dog-faced puffers, milk-spotted puffers, and snappers.

Shark Profiles: Brackish

Although many aquarist report keeping saltwater shark-like fish in estuary brackish tanks with success, in the beginning, keeping some form of shark catfish offers the greatest chance of success.

Australian Shark Catfish

The Australian Shark Catfish reaches a maximum length of 19.7 inches (50 cm). It does well with fish of an equal size or larger, and likes plenty of driftwood and rocks in which to hide.

This is an active species, which needs plenty of room to swim. It is dark gray overall with a bluish tint and a white underbelly. It accepts a wide variety of prepared and live foods, so it is an easy species to feed.

> ➤ Ideal conditions are 62.6-80.6° F / 17.0-27.0°C, pH 6.4-8.0.

Berney's Shark Catfish

Berney's Shark Catfish attains a maximum length of 15 inches (31.1 cm). It also requires tankmates of an equal or larger size, and likes plenty of hiding places.

An active swimmer, Berney's Shark is not a finicky eater. It is a silver to bronze fish that appears to be dark gray overall, with a paler underbelly.

> ➤ Ideal conditions are 68-82° F / 20.0-28.0°C, pH 6.4-8.0.

Columbian Shark Catfish

The Columbian Shark Catfish is a perfect tankmate for this kind of set up. It is a peaceful creature with new special needs. It reaches a manageable size of 10" (25.4 cm) when fully grown.

Although it will eat smaller species, it tends to get along well with fish of comparable size, especially if there are plenty of rocks and plants in the aquarium.

> ➢ Ideal water conditions are 74-79° F / 23.3-26.1°C, pH 7.0-7.5.

Chapter 6 - Shark Health and Breeding

The most serious health consideration in keeping sharks in a home aquarium lies in managing their diet. Many species will not eat when introduced to a new environment, or, aquarists who have failed to do their research think that, as carnivores, sharks will thrive on a protein-only diet.

This is far from the case, and you certainly can't keep a shark alive by just tossing some goldfish in the tank for a "snack" or expecting the animal to live on shrimp or squid only.

Smaller shark-like fishes do well with prepared pellet and/or flaked foods as well as freeze-dried bloodworms.

Larger, saltwater or "true" sharks have even more complex nutritional needs.

Saltwater sharks that are not receiving dietary supplementation can suffer from wasting and simply starve to death over time.

As discussed in Chapter 2, plan on giving your sharks a supplement like the Mazuri product Vita-Zu Shark/Ray Tablets to ensure the animal receives the full range of vitamins and minerals it requires.

Vitamin deficiencies in marine life can have severe consequences. A lack of vitamin B, for instance, can lead to curvature of the spine. This causes the shark to continuously swim in circles with its head slightly raised. The problem can be rectified by introducing vitamin B pellets in the food.

Damaging Shark Behaviors

Sharks can and do damage themselves in aquariums simply be engaging in harmful behaviors or falling victim to poor tank design.

Some smaller species, for instance, can be sucked into filtration intake tubes that are not covered with strainers. This is a particular problem with young Bamboo sharks due to their slender build.

It's also important to remember that many true sharks are omnivores who may eat unsecured pieces of aquarium equipment.

Something as simple as improper substrate will severely lacerate a shark's abdomen, especially if the species is benthic, or bottom dwelling.

Copper Sensitivity in Sharks

Although it is not true of all sharks, many species are highly sensitive to copper toxicity. The introduction of copper in any form will interfere with their feeding habits by weakening the shark's ability to locate food.

Research this specific issue with any shark you introduce to a tank, and read the ingredients of any medications or water treatment products you use to make sure no copper is present.

Common Tank Diseases in Sharks

The most common health problems for sharks are bacterial or viral in nature and manifest as visible skin lesions that may result in open sores and death.

Vibrio

This is a bacterial infection characterized by white skin lesions that erupt as sores that are highly susceptible to infection. It must be treated with chloramphenicol or tetracycline.

Tail and Fin Rot

Both of these conditions are common in bony fish, but can also occur in sharks. The rotting condition is a result of poor tank maintenance. The standard treatment is nitrofurazone.

Common Aquarium Diseases

The list of potential aquarium diseases is long and complex. Many issues stem from poor water chemistry, or from the presence of harmful bacteria.

Your best defense against tank diseases that may affect your sharks or shark-like fish is to have good reference sources on hand, and to participate in enthusiast communities online and off where you can describe symptoms and seek advice.

Some of the more common freshwater conditions include, but are not limited to:

- Anchor Worm
- Black Spot
- Clamped Fins
- Dropsy
- Fin Fungus
- Fin Rot
- Mouth Fungus
- Mouth Rot
- Pop Eye

Common saltwater conditions include, but are not limited to:

- Marine White Spot Disease (Ich)
- Marine Velvet
- Lateral Line Disease
- Cauliflower Disease
- Bacterial Diseases

Comprehensive reference sources for fish diseases include:

Fish Disease: Diagnosis and Treatment by Edward J. Noga

Handbook of Fish Diseases by G. Untergasser

Manual of Fish Health by Dr. Chris Andrews, Adrian Exell, and Neville Carrington

A-Z Tropical Fish Diseases and Health Problems by Peter Burgess

Sharks and shark fish are susceptible to any condition that can affect the larger tank.

Maintaining good water quality, minimizing stresses from major changes to the environment and proper maintenance (including regular cleaning) go a long way toward creating a balanced and healthy environment.

If a fish does become ill, immediately quarantine the animal in a separate tank to protect the remainder of your population and seek expert assistance in properly treating the tank to remove pathogens, bacteria, and potential parasites.

Shark Breeding in Home Aquariums

Space requirement pose the greatest hurdle to breeding sharks in home aquariums, followed closely by managing the animals' aggressive tendencies in relation to other tank inhabitants.

The best option for the hobbyist is to purchase a shark egg, which will hatch one to six weeks after introduction to the tank. This will allow you to raise your shark from birth to maturity without having to double or triple the size of the tank to accommodate a breeding pair and any offspring.

> ➢ Never buy a shark egg on impulse! Do your research first and understand exactly what you are doing.

> ➢ It is a myth that fish only grow to a size commensurate with the tank in which they live. If you buy a shark that as an adult will be 5 feet (1.52 meters) in length, the shark will grow to exactly that size.

Common Shark Eggs for Sale

Black Banded Cat Shark eggs are readily available for hatching in home aquariums, in part because live specimens of this species are notorious for refusing to eat when introduced to a tank.

If hatched in a tank, however, these sharks know no other way of life and will almost immediately accept frozen squid and other small pieces of food, often straight from your hand.

This shark reaches an adult length of 3-5 feet (0.91-1.52 meters) and will require a tank of at least 180 gallons (681.37 liters).

The species is aggressive, and must be carefully paired with tank mates to avoid predation.
Ideal water conditions include a temperature of 72°-78°F (22.22 – 25.55° C) with sg of 1.020 to 1.025.

- Note that there are other shark eggs available for sale, for instance the Bamboo shark. Always consider available space and existing tank population before deciding what species to hatch.

Tips for Hatching a Shark Egg

➢ Never, under any circumstances, allow the shark egg to be exposed to air. If an air pocket is allowed to form inside the egg, the shark will suffocate.

Always introduce a shark egg into a tank that is completely established with the best water parameters possible. Pay special attention to nitrate levels, as shark eggs are sensitive to an imbalance in this area of water chemistry.

Baby sharks need soft sand in the bottom of the tank to avoid abdominal injuries. You definitely do not want them hatching on crushed coral.

Because the eggs are translucent, you will be able to watch the shark using up the yolk inside the egg. This leads to a high degree of excitement on the part of most aquarists, especially if this is your first time hatching a shark egg.

> Resist the urge to help the shark hatch. Let the shark emerge from the egg on its own.

Do not be concerned if the young shark seems incredibly reluctant to eat at first. **This is normal**. Continue to patiently and consistently offer the baby food. It will eat, but it can take as long as a week.

Always have a cover on a tank where you are hatching a shark. Some juvenile sharks are jumpers, with other species retaining the tendency into adulthood.

Cost of Hatching a Shark

Expect to pay $40 to $80 (£25 - £51) for a Black Banded Cat Shark egg. The egg itself will be about 4 inches (10.2) cm and the shark upon hatching will be 5-6 inches in length (12.7-15.2 cm).

Afterword

When the famed cellist Pablo Casals was 95, a reporter asked him why he still practiced his instrument six hours a day. "Because I think I'm making progress," he replied.

Keeping an aquarium is much like playing a great instrument. When all the components of the composition are well measured and occupy their correct place, the result is a harmonious whole. One discordant element, however, can ruin the performance.

For an aquarist, that "wrong" note may be anything from incorrect water chemistry to aggressive algae growth. For a shark aquarist the discordance can stem from a host of bad decisions.

The most common of those is simply trying to raise a very large fish in a very small box.

If you are interested in keeping sharks in a home aquarium, take to heart the axiom, "Go big, or go home." Even the smallest species, those that don't grow to more than 2 feet (0.609 meters) in length need massive tanks.

Think back to the description of the minimum tank needed for the Bala Shark in Chapter 1:

"A tank that is 6' x 2' (1.82 m x .61 m)' will hold 180 gallons of water (681.37 liters) and, when fully equipped, will weigh more than 2,000 lbs. (907.18 kg)"

If that is not a tank you can afford or fit into your life, you shouldn't try to keep a Bala Shark, and you certainly should not give in to the myth that any fish will only grow to the size of the tank in which it is placed.

For many hobbyists who are interested in sharks, the sleek ferocity of a shark-like fish is sufficient to create the ambiance they desire in their tanks.

This class of fish, much more closely related to the minnow, is far easier to keep in a community tank at a greatly reduced cost both in terms of money and time.

This book is intended as a comprehensive overview of the subject of keeping sharks in a home aquarium.

If it has served to show you how little you know about keeping fish at this level, and encouraged you to learn more — and provided you with the right questions to ask — it has served its purpose.

Although the statistic is not widely known, more people keep fish in their homes than cats and dogs.

A beautifully designed tank is not only a fascinating environment in microcosm, but also a relaxing piece of living art that brings fluid beauty to your life.

Mankind undoubtedly has a love affair with the shark, a creature that seems both magnificent and powerful in its aloof and predatory existence.

Whether or not you are in a position to keep a shark as a pet is something only you can answer, but if the answer is yes, you are about to embark on nothing short of an experiment in world building.

You cannot live where a shark lives. You cannot breathe his atmosphere, or perhaps even understand the forces that drive his primitive but clever mind. This does not mean, however, that you cannot be his caretaker and derive hours of pleasure from his presence in your world.

Whether you choose to keep small, shark-like fish or true sharks, you, too, will find yourself resorting to that one word that is used over and over again in reference to these lords of the deep — awesome.

Afterword

Relevant Websites

Keeping Sharks in the Home Aquarium
http://www.fishchannel.com/fish-health/choosing-fish/keeping-sharks.aspx

Sharks for the Aquarium and Considerations for Their Selection
http://edis.ifas.ufl.edu/fa179

How to Set Up a Shark Aquarium
http://www.tankterrors.com/how-to-setup-a-shark-aquarium/

Aquarium Fish: The Epaulette Shark
http://www.advancedaquarist.com/2004/6/fish

LiveAquaria (Supplies and live fish.)
http://www.liveaquaria.com/

Saltwater Aquarium Guide - Sharks and Rays
http://www.saltwater-aquarium-guide.com/Sharks-and-Rays-thumbnails.htm

Sharks and Rays, Saltwater Fish Aquarium
http://www.aquacon.com/Sharks_saltwaterfish.html

The Top 10 Worst Tank Busters
http://www.ratemyfishtank.com/articles/146

Setting Up a Saltwater Aquarium
http://www.petco.com/caresheets/fish/SetUpSaltwaterAquarium.pdf

Setting Up a Freshwater Aquarium
http://www.petco.com/caresheets/fish/SetUpFreshwaterAquarium.pdf

Creating a Brackish Habitat Fish Aquarium
http://www.fishchannel.com/setups/special/creating-a-brackish-habitat.aspx

Water Chemistry
http://aquariuminfo.org/water.html

Frequently Asked Questions

I've decided I want to get a shark aquarium. What do I do first?

First, you decide how much money you can spend. If you want to keep a "true" saltwater shark, you're going to need a really large tank -- potentially as large as 180 gallons (681.37 liters) or more. That may well set you back as much as $1,350 (£860.79) for *just* the tank.

If you're going to keep a saltwater tank, you'll need a lot of additional equipment. So, decide what you can spend and then pick the kind of shark or shark-like fish you can successfully keep within the parameters of that budget.

Are aquariums a lot of work?

Keeping an aquarium, especially one for a sensitive fish like a shark, is labor intensive, but what's your definition of work?

If you love what you're doing and you're completely absorbed by all the intricacies of water chemistry and maintaining a healthy community of fish, it's not "work," it's a passion.

Most people don't realize that in the United States, there are more homes with aquariums than with cats and dogs.

If you've never kept an aquarium before, you do need to get yourself thoroughly educated first, including making friends with serious aquarists who can help you make good decisions from the start.

A beautifully designed aquarium is a piece of living art, and one that involves creating and maintaining a closed environment in microcosm. For many people, there's no more fascinating pastime.

I understand if I keep a shark I'm going to need a big tank. Will that add a lot of humidity to my house, and what about leaks and spills?

Every tank is subject to evaporation, but not enough to seriously elevate the humidity in your home.

For really big tanks, most aquarists take the precaution of installing an overflow box just in case. When you're dealing with large amounts of water, even the best designed piece of equipment can be subject to leaks and spills.

It's always a good idea to explore putting a rider on your homeowners insurance to cover this kind of damage when you get truly serious about keeping large tanks.

Do I really need to worry so much about tank size? Don't fish just grow to fit the space available to them and stop?

The idea that fish only grow to fit the space they have at their disposal is a huge myth.

If you're talking about keeping sharks, depending on the kind of shark you choose, you could be dealing with a creature that will reach 5 feet (1.524 meters) in length.

Getting the right size tank for the shark you are attempting to keep is absolutely critical. If you restrict these creatures to a smaller aquarium, you'll not only stunt their growth in ways that may deform them physically, but it's highly likely they won't survive at all.

As a beginner, should I really be thinking about a tank this large?

Actually, yes. While it may seem challenging to be talking about getting a tank as large as 180 gallons (681.37 liters) or more, it's actually much easier to maintain stable water chemistry in tanks that big.

Since water chemistry is usually what does a beginner in, starting large is to your advantage, especially if you take the time to learn about water, and get the right tools to monitor what's going on in your tank.

What are the real differences between saltwater and freshwater?

The biggest difference for the home aquarist is where these fish are captured.

Most freshwater fish are tank or pond raised. They tend to be a lot more tolerant of changes to their water chemistry. Saltwater fish are captured in the wild and they are highly sensitive to changes in their environment.

It's much more difficult to keep a saltwater tank, which is why many beginners start with freshwater, progress to a brackish tank, and then transition to a saltwater environment.

Just how hard is it to keep saltwater fish?

The important thing in a saltwater tank is to get your water chemistry right, and then to create a community of creatures that will get along.

Managing your population can actually be much more challenging than all the mechanics that go into designing your tank and getting the water balanced. This is particularly true when you keep sharks.

Some can only be kept with fish of comparable size, others will eat ever invertebrate you introduce to the tank, and some species have to live completely alone.

If you are going to keep saltwater fish, you have to learn their personalities and work out compatibilities in advance.

I'm trying to decide where to put my tank. Is it bad to put it in front of a window?

The first consideration with really big tanks is weight. A gallon of water weight 8 lbs. (3.628 kg), so do your math in advance.

A 180 gallon (681.37 liters) tank will weigh 1,440 lbs. or 653.17 kg. Chances are really good that's not going on the second story of your house. Worry about the foundation under your tank first.

Putting your tank directly in front of a window isn't a great idea. Uncontrolled sunlight can lead to runaway algae growth. It's much, much better to prevent algae than to try to get rid of it once it's become established.

You're better off picking a solid location and investing in good aquarium lights to create the "look" you're after. Also, if you put your tank in front of a window, you may have issues controlling the water temperature, which is a crucial element of tank maintenance.

I had no idea tanks weigh that much! How big can I go before my floor really does collapse?

For the most part, you're safe to put a 100 gallon (378.54 liters) tank just about anywhere in the house.

When you get into the range of 100 to 220 gallons (378.54 to 832.79 liters), the aquarium needs to be along a load-bearing wall perpendicular to the floor joists.

A tank of 220 to 400 gallons (832.79 to 1514.16 liters) will need to be placed on a reinforced floor. Anything above 400 gallons (1514.16 liters) needs to be sitting on a concrete slab.

(ALWAYS consult a structural engineer before installing a large aquarium. Not all construction is equal, and the slightest flaw in the integrity of your home or office building can result in disaster.)

Can you explain the difference in a "fish" tank versus a "reef" tank?

A "fish" tank is just what it sounds like -- all fish. You also have something called a FOWLR aquarium. That stands for "Fish Only With Live Rock," which means living coral is present to help with filtration and decoration.

A reef aquarium is carefully populated with peaceful fish that won't eat all the other life forms that can be placed inside like shrimp, anemones, crabs, sponges, snails, urchins, shrimp, starfish, crabs, duster worms and similar organisms that add variety and life.

Will a big tank run my electrical bill up?

This is an expense you'll have to calculate in operation. It's helpful if you use LED lights, since they will be running 8-11 hours a day. Most experts say that a 90 gallon tank (340.687 liters) draws 400-600 watts a day for the essential equipment and 200-700 watts for the lighting, but this can vary widely.

I'm already running a freshwater tank. Can it be converted to saltwater?

Yes, but you may want to just start a completely new tank. By the time you spend all the money for the additional equipment and get the water cycled (which can take up to two months), the conversion may not be worth it. You could be enjoying your freshwater fish while you design your new tank.

That being said, you can convert a tank to a brackish or "semi-saltwater" environment fairly easily and then proceed on to a full saltwater tank, but you need to think about what this will do to your existing population. It's not at all unusual for dedicated aquarists to have multiple tanks and tank types.

Are we talking about glass tanks or acrylic?

Most tanks under 300 gallons (1,135 liters) are made of glass because it's cheaper and more durable, plus these are still "off the shelf" aquariums.

Custom size tanks above 300 gallons (1,135 liters) are usually made of acrylic, which is more expensive, but it's also lighter and clearer. The big disadvantage is that acrylic scratches easily (although it can be buffed), so you have to be more careful when you clean.

Is it really practical to keep sharks in a home aquarium?

Yes. If you have the budget and the space, it's completely practical. Again, however, it's all a game of numbers. First decide how much you can spend, then look at the types of sharks that can successfully be kept in an aquarium of that size.

You may find that one of the many species of shark-like fish are a better fit for your circumstances, but don't regard that as a compromise. Although smaller, they are as streamlined and interesting as their larger cousins and are fascinating additions to any aquarium.

Aquarium Shark Species - Quick Reference

Freshwater Sharks

Bala Shark
semi-aggressive
maximum size 1'4" (40.64 cm)
minimum tank 70 gallons (264.97 liters)

Redtail Shark
semi-aggressive
maximum size 4" (10.16 cm)
minimum tank 50 gallons (189.27 liters)

Siamese Algae Eater
peaceful
maximum size 6" (15.24 cm)
minimum tank 30 gallons (113.56 liters)

Black Shark
aggressive
maximum size 2' (0.60 meters)
minimum tank 70 gallons (264.97 liters)

Albino Rainbow Shark
semi-aggressive
maximum size 6" (15.24 cm)
minimum tank 50 gallons (189.27 liters)

Chinese Hi Fin Banded Shark
peaceful
maximum size 18" (45.72 cm)
minimum tank 125 gallons (473.17 liters)

Silver Apollo Shark
passive
maximum size 9.8" (25 cm)
minimum tank 30 gallons (113.56 liters)

Rainbow Shark
semi-aggressive
maximum size 6" (15.24 cm)
minimum tank 50 gallons (189.27 liters)

Rose Line Shark
peaceful
maximum size 4.5" (11.43 cm)
minimum tank 50 gallons (189.27 liters)

Saltwater Sharks

Black Banded Cat Shark
aggressive
maximum size 3'6" (1.06 meters)
minimum tank 180 gallons (681.37)

Horn Shark
peaceful
maximum size 5' (1.52 meters)
minimum tank 1000 gallons (3785.41 liters)

Wobbygong Shark
aggressive
maximum size 4' (1.21 meters)
minimum tank 300 gallons (1135.62 liters)

Epaulette Shark
aggressive
maximum size 3'6" (1.066 meters)
minimum tank size 360 gallons (1362.75 liters)

Brackish Water Sharks

Australian Shark Catfish
semi-aggressive
maximum length 19.7" (50 cm)
minimum tank size 55-125 gallons (208.19 to 473.17 liters)

Berney's Shark Catfish
semi-aggressive
maximum length 15" (31.1 cm)
minimum tank size 55-125 gallons (208.19 to 473.17 liters)

Columbian Shark Catfish
peaceful
maximum length 10"(25.4 cm)
minimum tank size 55-125 gallons (208.19 to 473.17 liters)

Estimated Costs

Please note that all prices used in this book are estimates based on mid to upper-level equipment. Currency conversion rates fluctuate constantly. Use these prices as a starting point for your own research and comparisons, not as absolutes.

This list is not intended to be all-inclusive, but merely to bring into one location many of the costs or potential costs discussed in the text.

Keeping a large aquarium is a hobby that tends to grow on its own. One purchase leads to another, and the natural progression of a tank and its associated equipment is to become more complex and sophisticated not less so.

Always be prepared to spend more than you think you will spend!

Sharks

Prices are dependent entirely on species and availability. Many small shark-like fish can be purchased in the $5-$10 (£3-£6) range.

Medium-sized sharks under 2 feet (0.30 meters) are typically under $100 / £64.80.

Larger sharks can be anywhere from $300+ (£194 +) with some specimens selling for as much as $1000 (£648).

Examples of Tanks

20 gallon (75.7 liter) "kit"
$200-$250 / £127.52 / £159

50 gallon (189.27 liter) kit
$500 / £318.15

180 gallon (681.37 liter)
6' x 2' (1.82 m x .61 m)
Cost: $1,250 / £860

Larger and custom tanks should always be priced individually since they may include the cost of installation if structural reinforcement is needed to bear the considerable weight of the water.

For 500 gallons (1891.71 liters) and larger expect to pay at minimum $10,000 / £6,478 for a complete installation. Use this figure as a *starting estimate only. Costs vary widely by individual circumstance.*

Saltwater Equipment

Marine Salt, 5 gallons (18.92 liters) $50-$75 / £31 -£47

Protein Skimmer / 180 gallon (681.37 liter) capacity, $350 / £223

Powerheads / 180 gallon capacity (681.37 liter), $100-$500 / £63 - £318

RODI Unit / 180 gallon (681.37 liter) capacity $150-$250 / £95 - £159

Lighting $250-$500 / £159 - £318

Live Rock, 25 lbs. (11.33 kg) $75-$100 / £47 - £63

Heater / 180 gallon capacity (681.37 liter), $200 / £127

Chiller / 180 gallon capacity (681.37 liter), $500 / £318

Refractometer $150 / £95

Testing Kits (price per kit) $20-$40 / £12 - £25

Computer-based tank monitoring system (optional) $500-$1000 / £318 - £637

Sump / 250 gallon capacity (946.35 liter), $280 / £178

Auto Top Off System $175 / £111

7500 watt stand-by generator (optional) $700-$1000 (£444 - £637)

Overflow Box $150 / £95

Foods

Freeze Dried Mealworms .25 lbs. (113.39 grams) , $20 / £12

Marine pellet foods 10.58 oz. (300 grams), $35 / £22
(Prices for flaked foods are comparable.)

Prices for live foods for sharks like squid and shrimp vary widely by availability in your given location. Obviously regions nearer the ocean will have options for lower priced live food in bulk, which may be harder to obtain inland.

Shark-like fish in smaller aquariums can exist well on typical tropical fish pellets or flakes easily obtainable at "big box" retail pet stores in the $5-$10 (£3 - £6) range.

Nutritional Supplements

Mazuri Vita-Zu Shark/Ray Tablets
2 lbs. (.9 kg)
$110 / £71

Additional Potential Costs to Consider:

None of these costs are fixed or predictable and must be assessed on a per case basis.

- Structural changes to your home or office to accommodate the weight of a large tank.

- Moving / structural costs to relocate a tank if you change your residence or office location.

- Insurance on the tank itself to protect yourself against the loss of equipment and livestock in the event of a power failure or other disaster.

- Insurance for your home or office in the event of catastrophic tank failure resulting in water damage to the structure and its furnishings.

- Any potential medical costs associated with purchasing medicines or consulting with a tank specialist in the event of a widespread outbreak of disease or parasitical infestation.

Estimated Costs

Glossary

A

acidity - This is a measure of the pH level of the water. Although it is a common measurement taken of water quality, it is not as crucial as other aspects of water content like the level of ammonia present in tank water.

actinic lights - Fluorescent lights with a blue spectrum replicating the primary light in the ocean below a depth of 30 feet. This type of light is required by coral and other reef dwelling creatures.

activated carbon - Used in aquarium filters, this carbon-based material is highly absorbent. It does not remove ammonia or nitrite, nor does it soften the water, but it does help to control organic matter in the water.

adipose fin - A small fin located between the dorsal and caudal fins. It serves no apparent purpose.

adsorption - A chemical bonding between the chemical filtration media and water in an aquarium.

aerobic bacteria - Bacteria that can live or grow only in the presence of free oxygen.

air pump - A device that serves to oxygenate or aerate the water in the aquarium.

algae scraper - A tool used for the purpose of removing algae growth from the viewing areas of an aquarium.

algae - A large group of mainly aquatic plants containing chlorophyll that tends to proliferate as a nuisance in aquariums.

alkalinity - A measure of the acid-neutralizing capacity of water without a subsequent drop in pH levels. The more acid that can be added before a drop in pH is detected, the higher the alkalinity or buffering capacity of the water.

ammonia - In terms of aquarium maintenance, this is the major toxin that builds up in water due to the presence of fish excrement. It must be countered and neutralized by the correct action of the nitrogen cycle in the tank's bacteria.

anaerobic bacteria - Bacteria that can live or grow only when free oxygen is not present.

anoxia - A complete lack of oxygen.

anterior - Situated near to the front of the body or the head.

aquaculture - The cultivating of aquatic animals or plant for food or pleasure.

aquascaping - The craft of arranging the elements of an aquarium, including selecting the livestock, to aesthetically recreate an authentic underwater environment in closed conditions.

aquarist - A person who keeps an aquarium.

aquatic plant - Any plant that will grow fully or partially submerged in water.

autotrophic bacteria - Bacteria that need carbon dioxide to grow and reproduce.

B

barbel - A fleshy filament or "whisker" growing from the mouth of a fish. Typically seen in catfish.

beneficial bacteria - The bacteria in the nitrogen cycle that serves to convert ammonia, which is harmful to fish, to less harmful nitrate.

benthic - Happening on or existing at the bottom of a body of water.

biotope - The region of a habitat inhabited by or associated with a particular ecological community.

brackish - Slightly salty water present in places where fresh water sources meet the ocean, for instance estuaries.

C

carbonate hardness - An expression of the ability of water in your aquarium to absorb and neutralize acid.

carbon dioxide (CO2) - A colorless, odorless gas created by animal respiration and absorbed by plants during photosynthesis.

caudal fin - The tail fin on a fish.

chiller - Part of the life support system of an aquarium that serves to lower the temperature of the water below the ambient air temperature.

chlorination - The process of adding chlorine to water as a purification agent to make it fit for human consumption. Water used in aquariums must be de-chlorinated.

community tank - A tank designed to be inhabited with peaceful and compatible fish species.

cycling - The process of establishing the nitrogen cycle in a tank to create the presence of beneficial bacteria to convert toxic ammonia to nitrates. Without this cycle in place, an aquarium will not successfully support marine life.

D

damselfish - Any of a variety of small tropical marine fish of the family Pomacentridae.

deionization (DI) - A water purification process using ion exchange resins in combination with activated carbon and a bacterial filter to remove 100% of inorganic chemicals from water.

detritus - Dead material (either bacterial, plant, or animal) that can be degraded or mineralized by bacterial processes.

dorsal fin - The fin directly on top of the body, which, in a shark, can be seen protruding above the surface.

E

ecosystem - An interactive community of biological organisms and their physical environment.

elasmobranch - Sharks with cartilaginous skeletons like rays, skates, and sharks.

estuary - The mouth of a river that meets the ocean, characterized by "brackish" or semi-saltwater.

F

fluorescent light - Aquarium lighting fixtures that provide a broad spectrum of light for a relatively low cost.

G

glass aquarium - Aquariums made of glass and produced in standard sizes. Routinely sold in pet stores. Customized and high volume tanks are made of acrylic.

hang on the back filter - A filter that sits on the outside and back of an aquarium. These units are outfitted with a draw tube that brings water into the mechanism for filtration and then channels it back into the tank.

heater - A device, usually a glass tube, connected to an electrical socket for the purpose of controlling water temperature in an aquarium. Usually accurate within 2 degrees.

herbivore - An animal that eats plants as its principle food source.

hydrometer - An instrument used to measure the specific gravity of a fluid.

I

ions - elements or compounds (groups of elements) that have a negative or positive charge because of having gained or lost one or more electrons. See also anions and cations.

invertebrate - Animals that do not have a spine or backbone. Examples include starfish, clams, worms, and crags.

L

lateral line - A line of perforated scales running along the flank of a fish that are sensitive to vibrations in the surrounding water.

live rock - Marine rock or coral seeded with aquatic organisms. Used as decoration and biological filtration in reef and other kinds of saltwater tanks.

N

nitrification - The bacteriological process by which ammonia is converted to nitrite, and then nitrite to nitrate.

O

omnivore - An animal that eats both plant and animals as food.

P

predator - An animal that preys on other animals for food.

R

reverse osmosis (RO) - A method of water purification that uses high pressure and selective membranes to remove 100% of bacteria and 85% to 95% of inorganic chemicals.

S

salinity - A measurement of dissolved salts in water.

shark - A marine animal with a cartilaginous skeleton, a long body, prominent dorsal fin, and tooth-like scales. Of the subclass Elasmobranchii.

specific gravity - A measurement of the amount of salt in aquarium water.

substrate - The material at the bottom of an aquarium, typically gravel or sand.

sump - The box or container under a home aquarium that serves both as a water reservoir and a storage area for equipment.

T

territorial - Or relating to a real or perceived sense of ownership of an area of the land, sea, or immediate environment.

W

water quality - A term referring to the chemical composition of water at any given time.

Index

Lightning Source UK Ltd.
Milton Keynes UK
UKOW06f1845250815

257529UK00017B/505/P